FUCKING HISTORY

52 Lessons You Should Have Learned in School.

The Captain

© 2016 Rum Tongue Media Inc. All rights reserved. • ISBN-10: 0-692-79536-7 • ISBN-13: 978-0-692-79536-1

Definitely for Ashley.

TABLE OF CONTENTS

GETTIN' GHOSTED

Few things in life will make you feel as dumb as "getting ghosted." But you know what? Getting ghosted is a fucking blessing. Anybody who won't give you the courtesy of giving it to you straight is somebody you don't need in your life anyway. So, if you do get ghosted, keep doing your thing and make sure the person who ghosted you lives to absolutely fucking regret it. Be like Edith Wharton.

By the year 1905, Edith had already made quite a name for herself as an author and wordsmith. Sadly, her literary success did not carry into her marriage. And, like unhappily married people have been known to do, she had an affair. It began in 1906 with a kindred spirit she'd found in another writer by the name of William Morton Fullerton. Edith was head over heels for this guy and thought for sure he was the soulmate most people only ever dream of meeting. Unfortunately, the affair was short-lived when Fullerton disappeared on her sometime in 1908. Yep, he straight ghosted her ass.

Over the years, she did what she could to find him and make contact by writing hundreds of letters — yes, hundreds — in an attempt to get some closure, but Fuckboy Fullerton never bothered to even give her a response. Realizing love was dumb, and Fullerton was even dumber, she eventually gave up and got on with her life. In 1913, Edith divorced her husband and moved to France. There, she continued to write, and in 1916, she received a French Legion of Honor award for her work during the war.

In 1921, she became THE FIRST WOMAN EVER to win the Pulitzer Prize with her novel, "The Age of Innocence." Like a boss, she never remarried and spent the rest of her life living and writing in the French Riviera with her dogs, her garden, and her close friends. She even went on to receive three Nobel Prize nominations before her death in 1937.

And, what did Fullerton do with his life? Not much. His claim to fame was dating Edith, and the letters she wrote to him were eventually published in a book. Yeah, although he didn't respond, he received and saved every one — all 400 of 'em. (Huh, suddenly sending five texts in a row doesn't seem so bad.)

You see, getting ghosted is not the end of the world. If someone ghosts you, haunt their ass with your success. Or, just get, like, super fucking attractive. Either way, you win — they lose.

BORN TO KILL

Cold, calculated, patient, deliberate — no, I'm not describing a serial killer — I'm describing your girlfriend. Albeit, the characteristics of both are eerily similar, and this is why girls are scary as fuck. I know this, you know this, and the Soviets knew it back in the 1940s.

You see, during WWII, the Red Army recognized the close correlation between females and serial killers, so they began to heavily recruit women to become snipers. And, they were right to do so. Women were fucking naturals at that shit. They'd hand a gal a gun and tell her to pretend every Nazi soldier was her ex-boyfriend. Basically, anyone on the wrong end of her rifle didn't stand a chance. It was like handing a shark a fucking chainsaw and telling it to go make some sushi: It was a bloodbath. I mean, if you think your girlfriend is cunning and patient now because she'll wait 13 hours to pick a fight with you about something you said earlier in the day, imagine how cunning and patient she'd be in a life-or-death situation. Yeah, it's fucking sketchy. But also, it's pretty fucking awesome because tough girls are rad. During the war, the Soviets enlisted 2,484 female snipers. Who, together, killed an estimated 11,280 men — let's meet one of these ladies.

Allow me to introduce Lyudmila Pavlichenko, a.k.a. "Lady Death." Lyudmila was studying history at Kiev University when she volunteered for the Red Army in 1941. Think of it this way, while college students these days are taking it in the ass, both figuratively and literally — you know, with student loan interest rates, weird boyfriends, and whatnot — Lyudmila was out cappin' ass. Just how many asses did Lyudmila cap? 309. Yes, three hundred and fucking nine. Her kill count rivals your bank account.

Lyudmila was the definition of a strong, independent woman who didn't need a man. Besides, if she had one, she'd probably fucking kill him anyway. After the war, Lyudmila even went back to school to finish her college degree, picking up right where she'd left off. This, combined with her military prowess, makes her perhaps the most badass woman to have ever lived. I'd wife her in a heartbeat if she hadn't have died in 1974.

Guys, let this war story be a lesson to you: Your girlfriend was born with the ability to fucking kill you. So, be nice.

'TIL DEATH DO YOU PART (OR NOT)

You're a fucking catch. And, any dude you date should act like it. He's lucky to have you and he should be proud to show you off without caring about what others think or say. He should be exactly like King Pedro (a.k.a. Peter I of Portugal).

Here's his story: After the death of his first wife in 1345, which was an arranged marriage, Pedro married a young woman by the name of Inês de Castro — against his father's wishes. You see, Pedro was only a prince at the time, so whatever his father said was law. And, his father, King Afonso IV, absolutely did not approve of Pedro's marriage to Inês. Why all the commotion and disdain for the union? Well, Inês was not of royal blood; thus, she offered no strategic or political advantage to the kingdom or family reputation (which was a big deal back in the day).

Now, King Afonso wasn't about to just sit back and let his son disobey him like this. So, he hired three men to kidnap Inês, hold her hostage, and well, cut off her fucking head. (And you thought your dad overreacted when you brought your first boyfriend home in high school.)

After learning what his dad had done, Pedro swore revenge. But again, he was still just a little prince at the time and didn't hold the power necessary to retaliate against his father. However, fortunately for Pedro, he didn't have to wait too long to inherit that power. King Afonso died in 1357, just a couple years after Inês' murder, and Pedro became the new King of Portugal. King Pedro's first order of business? Make good on his revenge promise — but how?

Well, he tracked down the three men his father had hired to kill Inês and had their hearts removed while they were still alive. Because, as he claimed, they had done the same to him when they killed Inês. (Pretty emo move if you ask me, but I can respect it.) Then, Pedro had Inês' body exhumed, dressed in royal cloth, and seated next to him on a throne as the rightful queen. Yeah, that's how proud Pedro was of her. Dead, without makeup, and with no fucking eyebrows (but probably with some kick-ass skeleton contouring), Pedro still wanted to show her off. So much so that he forced the entire kingdom to form a line, bow, and kiss her bony, dead hands. Now THAT'S a dude who's proud of his relationship and truly doesn't give a fuck about what others think.

(It's worth noting that Pedro went on to become a complete psychopath of a king, known for his affinity for torture, brutality, and living heart removal. But, let's not focus on that — let's focus on how proud he was to be married to Inês, and how little he cared about the opinions of others.)

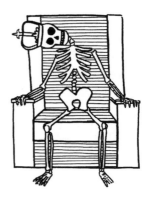

TIMELESS BEAUTY

"Resting Bitch Face." This term has been floating around a lot the last few years, making its way into a slew of selfies, memes, and pop-culture articles. But, it's nothing new. The art of looking like a handsome bitch, dick, or asshole has been around since the beginning of time. Why? Because there's a certain level of respect, mystery, and intrigue that comes from looking seductive, yet absolutely terrifying. For centuries, women have used RBF to lure kings from their thrones, and those kings, in turn, have used RBF to intimidate and conquer rival lands.

The history of RBF is firmly rooted in honor, attraction, and self-respect. You see, throughout history, self-respect has always been closely related to smiling (or the lack thereof). Aside from the obscenely long exposure times required for old photography to work properly, you don't often see people smiling in old photos or paintings as it was considered foolish to pose with a smile on your face. Because, well, it was probably fake. To smile for a portrait was not an accurate depiction of emotion. You were smiling just to smile, not because you were genuinely happy. You know, like when you fake a smile for your boss in order to conceal your complete mental breakdown.

In fact, it was Mark Twain (perhaps you've heard of him) who said, "A photograph is a most important document, and there is nothing more damning to go down to posterity than a silly, foolish smile caught and fixed forever." In my opinion, no truer words have ever been spoken.

Except maybe the infamous TLC line, "Don't go chasing waterfalls." Which, oddly enough, is also a statement concerning self-respect. Huh, weird.

Now, the next time someone asks you why you don't smile in photos, you have some history to school them with that supports your decision. Tell them you're doing it for your posterity.

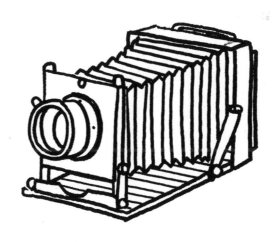

TWO'S A COUPLE, THREE'S A CROWD

The ultimate goal of dating: Finding your equal. Someone equally as fun, equally as cool, or simply, equally as fucked up as yourself. And, every now and then, you encounter a couple that has successfully done this. These couples give you hope. Hope that you might also one day find a counterpart. Not to mention, couples that successfully find their equal are usually "the cool couple." So even your single friends will be happy for you because you're still fun to hang out with since you don't have to change who you are to be around your friends and your boyfriend/girlfriend at the same time.

Now, no matter how unappealing you think a certain aspect of yourself might be, there's no need to change it. Trust me, there's someone out there — just like you — who will dig that part of your character. Let's discuss this further with a historical example.

In 1860, on the French Caribbean island of Martinique, Blanche Dumas was born with a condition known as Tripedalism (three legs), as well as a condition known as Uterus Didelphys (double sex organs). Which means, you guessed it, two vaginas. (And here you are, worried about your thigh gap with just one vagina. Shit, you have it easy.) Now, you'd think with her condition she was doomed to be alone, right? Wrong. Enter Juan Baptista dos Santos from Portugal (born 1843), who, guess what, also happened to have been born with Tripedalism AND Diphallia (three legs, two dicks). I'm not making this shit up, you can Google it, but I don't recommend it.

Well, after Blanche and Juan learned about each other through the local freak show circuit, the two obviously had to meet. Basically, one was peanut butter, the other was jelly, and together, they made one hell of a freaky fucking sandwich. It's unknown how long the romance lasted, but it goes to show you, there's somebody out there for everyone.

Stop changing yourself for the people you date, because there really is someone out there who will dig everything about you — even an extra leg. And for those of you who have found that person, be glad you met online and not at a local freak show. (Although, freak shows tend to have fewer weirdos.)

STAGE FRIGHT, DIVORCE FIGHT

If it seems like marriage isn't taken seriously these days, that's because it's not. But during the Middle Ages, marriage was ABSOLUTELY serious shit. When you said, "till death do us part," it really meant till fucking death. If you wanted out of a marriage, you pretty much had to wait for your spouse to die, or handle your shit and kill them yourself. Divorce simply wasn't an option.

Plain and simple, if you didn't like the way your husband treated you, you had to poison that fucker's food. I know this sounds morbid, but during this time period, we're talking about a lot of arranged, underage marriages put in place for political motives, and/or creepy, brother-sister marriages set up in order to maintain the family bloodline. These marriages were fucking hell, and the women were fucking miserable because the Catholic Church simply wouldn't allow for divorce. Basically, your life was over if your uncle's 57-year-old friend wanted to marry you and your dad decided it would be good for the family.

But, this all changed in mid 16th-century France with the introduction of the French Impotence Courts. Finally, women had a way out. If you could prove your husband's dick was as limp as hot spaghetti, the church would grant you a divorce. How would a woman prove this? Easy. She'd bring that freckly, old fuck before a judiciary panel and they'd watch him jerk off — and if he couldn't do it — she was free to begin her new life as a single lady. *"Oh my God, look who's single again — you are!"*

Let's think about this for a minute though. As a dude, this would totally fucking suck, because "stage fright" is a very real thing. Realizing this, the French added a second part to the impotence proceedings. If the husband — a.k.a. "the owner of the broken dick in question" — wanted help to prove the fact that his junk actually worked, he could request his wife take part in the act as well. The panel would assume their position, accused husband and angry wife would assume theirs, and that was that. Time to lay some butter on that bread and see who's lying.

So, the next time you think the world we live in today is sick and wrong, think about this: At least you can end a marriage without answering the bone phone in front of a judge.

MEOWLESS AND BROWLESS

You think you love your cat? Wrong. You might "like" your cat, but you definitely don't love it — at least not as much as the Ancient Egyptians loved theirs. Seriously, the Egyptians fucking LOVED cats. They liked dogs too, but cats were the real deal. They adorned their cats with jewels, fed them as royalty, and treated them better than most people — like you probably do — because lots of people suck.

Personally, I think cats are fucking weird; they freak me out. When a cat looks at you, it could be thinking about cuddling up under your arm, or eating your face while you sleep. That's how unpredictable they are. And, that unpredictability is probably what made the Egyptians love them so much, because the Ancient Egyptians themselves were fucking psychos. But, Egyptian torture techniques are a topic for another day. Back to the kitty cats . . . okay, maybe just one: The Egyptians used to strip people naked, cover them in milk and honey, tie them between two boats floating in stagnant water, and simply leave. Use your imagination. HINT: Lots of hungry-ass bugs live around stagnant water, and hungry-ass bugs love milk, honey, and holes — almost as much as the Egyptians loved their cats.

Obviously, when a cat died, the Egyptians were fucking devastated. And they chose to mourn their loss very publicly. First, they would shave off their eyebrows to symbolize the loss of their furry pet. When the meows go, the brows go. That's just the Egyptian way. The cat was then mummified and placed into the family tomb. The grieving period lasted until your eyebrows grew back. (Which takes fucking FOREVER, by the way.)

Damn, the Egyptians make your weak-ass social media posts about how much you love your pet look pretty lame. All I'm trying to say is: If you really love your cat, you'll shave off your eyebrows when the unfortunate day comes. I mean, it's not like I'm suggesting anything too crazy — you already look like you don't have eyebrows when you take off your makeup anyway.

A CATFISH CRUSADE

"Catfishing," it's nothing new. Sure, the internet made it easier, online dating made it extremely prevalent, and some network even made a TV show, but catfishing has been around for thousands of years. Let's go back to a time when two major forces — the Persians and the Egyptians — ruled much of the civilized world to learn more about how it all began.

In an effort to keep peace between the two kingdoms, the Persian Emperor, Cambyses II, asked Pharaoh Amasis II to arrange the marriage of himself to the pharaoh's daughter. But, Amasis knew if he did this, his daughter would be treated as simply another notch in Cambyses' belt rather than an actual wife. Cambyses didn't exactly have a reputation as a respectful dude. In fact, he was known as quite the womanizing douche. So, Amasis sent a pharaoh's daughter — just not his daughter. Instead, he sent the daughter of his predecessor, the deceased Pharaoh Apries. Thus, the first recorded catfish in history was underway. The year was approximately 526 B.C. (You see, catfishing has been around for-fucking-ever.)

When Cambyses realized he'd been deceived, he was furious and immediately declared war on the Egyptian kingdom. Now, things didn't exactly happen as quickly back then as they do today, so by the time Cambyses had gathered his forces and made the trek to Egypt, Pharaoh Amasis was already dead. It was now the duty of Amasis' son, Pharaoh Psametik III, to defend against Cambyses' Catfish Crusade of 525 B.C. — otherwise known as "The Battle of Pelusium."

So, just how does one go about seeking revenge after being catfished? Well, with a cat fight of course. No, really, the reason Cambyses took so long to organize his retaliation was because he needed to collect a shitload of cats. He knew the Egyptians worshipped cats (we just discussed this), so Cambyses had his army use cats as shields. His men literally marched into battle carrying cats. And, fearful of harming the very animals that represented their Goddess Bastet, the Egyptians refused to fire arrows or throw spears at the Persian invaders. Which, of course, led to an absolute fucking slaughter and decisive Persian victory. (Seriously, why are cat people so fucking weird?)

Now, after you text your friend about the history lesson you just learned, get off your phone. For real, stop using your phone — or your cat — as a shield to avoid human interaction. Go the fuck outside.

APPLE ALLURE

Okay, there's no point in beating around the bushel, so we're going to get right into this one. Back in 19th-century Austria, women used to place an apple slice in their armpit before taking to the dance floor. (Why the armpit? Well, because it's within easy reach, and also because a dress with pockets looks fucking homely.) The lady would keep her apple slice warm as she danced the night away with a multitude of male suitors. When the music stopped and the night was over, she'd present her sweaty pit fruit to whichever man she was interested in further pursuing. This is where it gets really fucking weird, because if the guy shared her interest, he'd eat her salty slice. Thus, signifying he was into her.

Now, I don't know about you, but I would never eat someone's hot fruit on a first date — that's some third-, fourth-, or maybe even fifth-date kind of shit. However, I do respect the talent it must have required to keep an apple slice from falling out of your armpit while you twerk the night away. Shit, these women might as well have put some flour and an egg in their armpit along with that apple — while they heated things up on the dance floor, their body could have heated up an apple pie. *"Impressive multi-tasking, Elizabeth."*

There's actually a lot we can learn from this apple tradition; it might even be worth bringing back. Like my grandma always said, "The fastest way to a man's heart is through his stomach." I mean, not only is this technique a great way to offer the hungry, drunk guy a snack after he's finished dry humping your leg, it's clearly an even better way to gauge his level of interest in you. Because if a dude is willing to eat something you made with your own sweat and body heat, he really likes you — maybe even "like-likes" you . . . keep your fingers crossed.

So, the next time you go out with your girls, leave your purse in the car. Your body has all the curves and snack pockets you need.

SOBRIETY SUCKS

Every girl loves wine. And, that's cool. It's good to have a hobby. But, did you know, in Ancient Rome women were forbidden to drink wine? Yeah. For-fucking-bidden — that's just crazy.

In fact, drinking wine was considered such a serious offense, a man was allowed to divorce his wife if he caught her guzzling the Grigio, chugging the Chianti, swigging the Soave, drinking the . . . okay, I think you get the point. A housewife drinking wine was what the Romans considered a "major fault." Drinking wine ranked right up there with adultery because the Romans believed drinking wine led to bad decisions . . . like adultery. (FYI - The last known Roman divorce on basis of a "wine-o wifey" was sometime during the 2nd century B.C.)

First off, duh, of course drinking wine leads to bad decisions. That's why drinking wine and other intoxicants is good for you: It helps you learn from your mistakes. Second, fuck the Romans. If they were so worried their wife having a drink would cause her to cheat on them, maybe they should have gotten their priorities in order and stopped being such a fucking dick. And, I don't know, maybe hit the gym every once in a while. They could have wrestled with some dudes in the courtyard or something to ensure they looked like one of those buff-ass statues all over town. There's a reason women loved watching the sweaty gladiators kill each other: muscles. You think Hercules had to worry about his lady getting drunk and falling on some other dude's dick? No, Hercules was buff as hell. He looked like his dad created him using Photoshop and a chisel.

Anyway, just when you thought you knew everything about wine, you just learned something new. I guess even wine snobs can benefit from some history every now and then. You're welcome. Now, open a bottle, or a box (depends on what your last paycheck looked like) and celebrate your newfound drinking knowledge.

TOO MANY TO NAME

So, just how many dogs is too many? Three? Four? FIVE? For the sake of time, let's settle on "five." I mean, sure, by today's standards, that's a lot of dogs to own. But when we look back through history, that's nothing compared to the number of dogs owned by Kublai Khan. However, before we talk about his pups, I want you to learn more about who Kublai Khan was.

From May 5, 1260, to February 18, 1294, Kublai Khan was the Supreme Khan of the Mongols, the first emperor of the Yuan Dynasty, AND the Emperor of China. (Pretty impressive résumé.) Essentially, he was the fucking man. So what does the fucking man do? Well, he owns a lot of fucking dogs. How many? Five thousand. Yeah, you read that right, Khan owned FIVE THOUSAND mastiffs. Seriously, take a moment to imagine what a pack of 5,000 dogs looks like . . . I don't know how you're picturing it, but for me, I imagine looking at a pack of 5,000 dogs is a lot like looking at a bathtub filled with 5,000 bags of M&M's: You know it's a bad idea, but for some reason, you still want 'em all.

Now, if Khan had owned 5,000 cats, it wouldn't have been nearly as impressive or intimidating. It would have completely changed the way his rivals viewed him. Instead of looking like a badass, he'd look like a crazy, lonely weirdo. Basically, what I'm saying is: If you know you're doomed to be single your entire life, don't banish yourself to the life of a crazy cat lady. Instead, be a damn cool dog owner. With a lot of dogs, people won't even feel sorry for you. They'll just be like, "Damn, what a badass."

And, instead of looking like you belong on one of those TV shows about hoarding, you'll look like someone who's anything but boring.

What are you waiting for? Go fill the backseat of your car with beef jerky, drive slowly around town with the doors open, and start collecting strays — because it's going to take you a while to get to 5,000 and become Kublai Khan-level cool.

BLONDES HAVE MORE FUN

Did you know the blonde allele is so recessive and rare that only two percent of the world's population has naturally blonde hair? Well, it's true. So throughout the years, those outside of the allele in-crowd, have tried some pretty weird shit in pursuit of golden locks. Back in the day, you couldn't exactly walk to the store and buy an eight-dollar box of do-it-yourself bullshit. Really, eight dollars? C'mon, of course that product is garbage. If you're trying to go blonde, put up the money to have it done by a professional. You'll be glad you did when you end up looking like an ice princess instead of the fucking pumpkin that was used to make Cinderella's carriage. It's your choice: Do you want to be a princess, or do you want to be a Halloween decoration? While you think about that, let's discuss some old-timey hair dying techniques.

In Ancient Rome, women attained the golden glow with the use of pigeon shit. In Renaissance Venice, they used horse urine. Why? Well, like most permanent hair dye, both of these items contain ammonia. Now, I'm not exactly sure how effective these organic products were (or still are), but what could possibly be more enjoyable than washing your hair with animal excrement? These blondes really were having more fun. And if they weren't, at least their beauty products were made by animals instead of being tested on animals — right?

Speaking of blondes having more fun, in Ancient Greece, prostitutes were easy to spot because they usually wore blonde wigs. I guess you could say those blondes were also having more "fun."

Anyway, don't let anyone tell you that you're a dumb blonde anymore, because you just learned some blonde history. You're welcome.

LEAVE AN IMPRESSION

To further elaborate on the brief mention of Greek prostitution in the previous lesson — do you really think Cinderella was the first girl to purposely leave something behind in order to get a text back? Nope. People have been using that trick for centuries. In fact, the prostitutes of Ancient Greece had the art of the leave-behind mastered. They would walk around wearing sandals with the phrase *"ΑΚΟΛΟΥΘΕΙ"* imprinted on the soles. Translation? "Follow me."

As they walked, this message was left behind in the sand for horny Greco-Roman guys. The prostitutes were literally leaving a trail of grammar breadcrumbs that, if followed, led to an expensive good time. (NOTE: Paying for sex is probably the only way a dude wearing flip-flops will ever get laid. So of course prostitution was popular in Greece, every guy was constantly wearing a toga and sandals.)

So, how does this all apply to you? Simple. Leaving shit behind is a solid dating strategy.

Now, it's worth mentioning, single parents have a major advantage at this game. Because I guarantee, if you leave a kid behind after a first date, you'll definitely be getting a text back to come get him or her — quickly. Hell, you can even use your kid to break the ice with new people as well. It happens like this: You sit down next to an attractive guy or gal at your favorite restaurant, you fake like you're getting an important phone call, then you go outside to "hear better." You casually walk towards your car like you forgot your child and wait for your target to take the bait.

"Oh my God, thank you so much. I can't believe I left my kid behind. I could sure use someone like you in my life. Wanna date?" Yeah, it's that fucking easy.

Don't have kids? Don't worry. If you're creative enough, you can think of a leave-behind equally as effective as a human child. Trust me, I do it all the time. And, "No," leaving your phone number on the receipt at brunch this weekend in hopes of your server calling you is not a smooth move. Leave something they will actually remember — like a puppy, or your fucking pants.

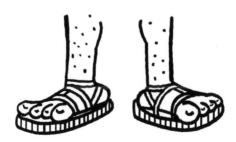

PIGGYBACKS SAVE LIVES

You haven't truly lived until you've given a really drunk person a piggyback. Especially if you're equally as drunk yourself. Because nothing will bring you closer as friends, or strengthen your relationship more than stumbling around city streets together like conjoined, drunk idiots — too dumb to request a car, too drunk to give a fuck. Seriously, a good piggyback can be a lifesaver, both figuratively and literally. Figuratively, in the sense that you don't want to scuff the new Louboutins you just spent half of your paycheck on; and literally, like what the men of Weinsberg, Germany, experienced during King Conrad III's siege on their castle.

You see, King Conrad was not a patient man — and on one particular day in 1140 — he'd grown tired of his failed attempts to take Weinsberg Castle. So, rather than continue fighting and failing, he offered the castle inhabitants a deal: Stop resisting and he'd allow all the women to go free, along with whatever valuables they could carry on their backs. As for the men, they were fucked. He would behead them all. Well, as any man should do in order to protect his wife, all of the men agreed to the deal and stopped fighting — sacrificing themselves and accepting their fate as dead men. (To their wives, I like to imagine they all looked like Channing Tatum during this moment: Just super noble and handsome.)

Now, here's where the story gets good. Adhering to the king's offer, the women loaded up their backs with their most-prized possessions: their husbands. I'm sure a few women opted to leave theirs behind, but for the most part, each woman carried her man out of the castle. Piggybacking them to safety. Damn, those are some tough chicks. They didn't even have CrossFit back then. Anyway, when the king's troops saw what was happening, they were fucking furious. But, King Conrad was quite amused with the cleverness the women showed. So he replied to his troops, "A king should always stand by his word." And, he did, allowing all of the men and women of Weinsberg Castle to live.

After this event, the women of Weinsberg became known as "Treue Weiber," meaning "loyal women." And, the castle grounds were later renamed to "Weibertreu."

Well, there you have it, dudes. Treat your ladies right. You never know when you might need her to carry your dumb ass to safety. Or, at least help you onto the couch when you've had too much to drink.

TEMPER TANTRUMS

Now, there's "overreacting," and then there's OVER-FUCKING-REACTING. You all know what I'm talking about. Overreacting can simply be defined as "going too far." For girls, it's the difference between telling your boyfriend to fuck off, and using scissors to actually cut the words "fuck" and "off" into all of his favorite t-shirts. (Funny, but depending on what he actually did, you might be going too far.) For guys, it's the difference between being slightly annoyed that your girlfriend still talks to her ex, and telling her if she doesn't delete her account or block him immediately — you're done. Relax, dude. In the age of the internet and social media, nobody is able to completely disconnect from an ex unless they move to North Korea or go to prison. Just accept the fact that you're not the only guy on the planet and stop acting like a petty dumbass.

Basically, don't be like Ibrahim "The Mad." You see, Ibrahim I was Sultan of the Ottoman Empire from 1640 to 1648, and was quite the womanizer. And, like most womanizers, he was extremely insecure, quick-tempered, and required the constant validation of new females — evident with his obscenely large harem of 280 women. So what does this story have to do with overreacting? Well, I'm about to tell you.

When one of Ibrahim's concubines decided to sleep with someone other than Ibrahim (probably some handsome, cool dude like your girlfriend's ex), Ibrahim "The Insecure" lost his fucking shit. He threw a tantrum like no other and had 278 (some sources say all 280) of his concubines bound with rope and drowned in the Bosphorus Strait as punishment for the one disobeying him and the others protecting her. That's pretty much the historical equivalent of forcing your girlfriend to delete her social media accounts. Because, let's be honest, without social media, you might as well be dead.

Well, you just learned some history. You also learned that Ibrahim was a fucking dick. So, yeah, don't be that guy.

REINVENTING YOURSELF

Shit happens — relationships end, jobs are lost, and well, life doesn't always go the way you'd planned. Maybe you were a super cute kid growing up, and thought for sure you were destined for a career in modeling, but the blooming teenage years were harsh. (Let's just say you emerged looking more like a caterpillar and less like a butterfly.) That's life. Sometimes things happen that force you to look at your alternatives in order to continue moving forward. And, THAT is fucking great. It's an opportunity to reinvent yourself and become even cooler than you were before.

Going back to the example of the formerly cute kid turned high school hunchback, if life deals you a caterpillar face, use those bug eyes to your advantage. You could easily become an actor. One who makes tons of money playing a creepy stalker, a praying mantis, or a serial killer. My point is: With an open mind, it's never "the end." Take for example, King Eric VII of Denmark, also known as Eric of Pomerania, or Erik av Pommern. (Yeah, lots of alternative spellings here.)

You see, Eric was the King of Denmark from 1389-1442, the King of Sweden from 1396-1439, and also the King of Norway from 1396-1439. (Quite the curriculum vitae.) Unfortunately, despite being a charming and charismatic leader, a series of public rebellions began during the 1430s. So, in 1439, Eric simply said, "Fuck you, dorks — I'm out." Fed up with the rebellions, he went on strike and moved into his secluded Castle Visborg on the island of Gotland. (Kind of like Elsa's ice palace.)

When it became clear he was in no hurry to come back, the nobles of the countries he'd left behind called his bluff and deposed him as their king — not exactly the idea Eric had in mind. But, he wasn't the kind of guy who easily gave up. So, he took advantage of his leadership experience in order to reinvent himself into the perfect pirate. And, for the next 10 years, he kidnapped ships, held ports for ransom, and did all sorts of piratey things in order to maintain his lavish lifestyle and once again say, "Fuck you," to his former countrymen. Talk about taking control of your life. Bravo, Eric . . . bra-fucking-vo.

I want you to remember this story the next time life gets shitty or something doesn't go as planned. Use it as an opportunity to become something better — and despite what your teachers told you growing up — YOU CAN become a fucking pirate.

A TRULY LOYAL ROYAL

Popular culture has given us a lot of bullshit over the past few years: cinnamon-flavored whiskey, pumpkin-spice everything, and the general notion that "hoes ain't loyal." I get it, that was a catchy song — but if you're reading this, and you're a guy — it's time you move on from that mindset. Trust me, there are still some women, like Olga of Kiev, out there. You just have to be worthy and ready to actually date one.

Olga was a princess during the 10th century in an area now divided between Ukraine and Russia. And don't let the name "Olga" fool you — she was absolutely fucking gorgeous. She was also extremely loyal to her family, her country, and her man. So, naturally, tons of dudes wanted her. So much so that the jealousy of other men eventually led to the assassination of her husband, Igor of Kiev, who was killed by the rival Drevlians in hopes of convincing Olga to marry one of their own, Prince Mal. But, Olga didn't want anything to do with their Drevlian bullshit. She had her man, she lost her man, and her son was now the only man who mattered in her life. She would rather die — sad, wrinkly, alone, and smothered in fucking cats — than ever marry Prince Mal's Drevlian ass.

So when Mal sent 20 of his finest negotiators in an attempt to persuade Olga to accept his marriage proposal, she had all 20 of them buried alive. When he sent a group of nobles as a follow-up, Olga had them locked in a bathhouse and burned alive. Olga then pretended to apologize by inviting all the Drevlians to a party. At that party, she had her army kill

5,000 men — but she wasn't done yet. Olga then invaded the Drevlians' lands and had her army burn down every fucking house. (In case you haven't caught on, Olga really liked fire.) I think it was about this time Prince Mal realized Olga was too much woman for him and he gave up trying to pursue her.

Olga continued to rule over Kievan Rus' as a single, independent woman from 945 to 963 on behalf of her son until he was old enough to rule alone.

Now, ladies, if a guy ever questions your loyalty or calls you a "ho," be like Olga and burn his fucking house down.

FEAR OF MISSING OUT

FOMO. For those of you who didn't read the title of this lesson, that's short for, "Fear of Missing Out." FOMO can apply to nearly every aspect of life. Unfortunately, with jobs, family, and other responsibilities, you'll never be able to experience everything — you're going to miss out — often. That's just part of being a functioning adult. But you know what? It's not that bad. Sure, it can be frustrating, but not nearly as frustrating as what happened to former horse trainer, turned jockey, Frank Hayes.

You think missing last Friday's party was bad? Well, this poor bastard missed out on the biggest moment in his racing career. He won, but wasn't there to enjoy it. How does that fucking happen? I'll tell you. On June 4, 1923, Frank suffered a fatal heart attack midway through a race at New York's Belmont Park. He died, but his horse kept running and actually won the fucking race. The weirdest part: Nobody even noticed Frank was dead until afterward. The officials went over to congratulate him on his first-ever career win and found a corpse saddled in. Frank's dead, lifeless body was just bobbing around on top while the horse did all the work. (You know, like a terrible sexual partner: Physically they're there, but other than that, they're fucking lifeless.)

Talk about missing out. The greatest accomplishment of Frank's life, and he wasn't even there to enjoy it. Hopefully, somebody in Heaven threw him a celebration party.

Anyway, FOMO sucks, but as long as you're there for the big, important moments of your life — like winning your first race — it's okay to miss a party here and there. Prioritize, and pray you don't die when something really cool actually happens.

Well, now that you've learned something new, you should go out and experience something new. Sign up for a pottery class or some shit. You wouldn't want to miss out on the opportunity to make a cool mug or something, would you?

FAKE IT, SEE HOW THEY TAKE IT

We all know what it's like to try and interpret someone's body language, analyze their subtle cues, and read between the lines of each and every text message. Why do we do this? Because we want to know if they feel the same way about us as we do about them. Do they like me? Do they *really* like me? Plain and simple, dating is confusing. And now, with social media, texting, dating apps, and a variety of other confusing modern-day creations, the relationship Rubik's Cube is more complicated than ever before.

Sure, you can spend your time Googling lists and articles about how to tell if a guy or girl likes you. Personally, I like what Lord Timothy Dexter did to shake up the New England socialite society of the 18th century: He faked his own death.

Not a big deal; well, until you consider he was married at the time AND attended his own funeral as one of the nearly 3,000 guests. (Attending my own funeral is *definitely* on my bucket list.) But, out of those thousands in attendance, Mr. Dexter was really only concerned about the reaction of one individual in particular: his wife, Mrs. Dexter.

Anyway, guess what? She didn't even cry at the funeral. WHAT THE FUCK? So, the not-so-dead Timothy was forced to reveal himself. After confronting Mrs. Dexter about her lack of emotion, he proceeded to publically cane her. Which is pretty fucked up because it's exactly what it sounds like. I mean, I would have just told her it was over and I was taking the dogs (maybe even the kids), but Tim had a bit of a temper. Not too surprising — it takes someone pretty unstable to fake their own death.

However, what he did was actually kind of brilliant. It's a great way to tell if somebody shares the same level of devotion that you do. So, the next time you have questions about the seriousness of your relationship, don't eliminate faking your death as an option . . . it's fucked up, but it's effective.

SUPPORT YOURSELF

Here's a little fact you probably didn't know about boob control: That elastic-clasp bra strap you've been taking for granted all these years was invented by none other than the famous author Samuel L. Clemens.

Filed for patent in 1871, Clemens was more than ecstatic — and far from humble — about his incredible elastic creation. How do we know this? Well, because he wrote the following phrase on the patent application: "The advantages of such an adjustable and detachable elastic strap are so obvious that they need no explanation." He claimed the invention was useful for vests, pants, and any other garment requiring adjustment. Fortunately, the "other garment" category really took off. Thank God, right? That's the category that needed Clemens' creation the most.

As a girl, could you imagine trying to control your sweater puppies without this device? As a guy, well, you can thank Samuel for helping you easily let the dogs out. (And, dudes, don't act like you're fucking smooth. I guarantee you've been so excited and shaky, you've considered using scissors; trembling like a Chihuahua about to take a piss. "Oh my God, I'm gonna see a nipple." Relax, Peter Pan, maybe if you spent less time with your Lost Boys you wouldn't be so intimidated by the female form. You still think growing up is stupid?)

Anyway, before this device, women had the choice of either wrapping up like a mummy, forcing their girls into a corset, or simply saying, "Fuck it," and walking around flapping like the ears of a Bloodhound. (Are you getting tired of my dog references yet? Good, because I'm not either.) I guess all I'm trying to say is: Long before Victoria had a secret, Samuel Clemens had a vision.

Oh, and did I mention Clemens' pen name was Mark Twain? Yeah, THE Mark Twain. The same dude who wrote that book about Tom and Huck not giving a fuck and running away to an island. You also read about him earlier in this book. Anyway, take it easy and don't let the dogs out. (Unless I'm invited.)

SHOW SOME RESPECT

Moving on to another story about boobs, let's be honest, everybody loves them. I mean, except for some absolute prudes, everyone enjoys a good set of boobs.

Seriously, girls like their own boobs, guys like their girl's boobs, and girls like other girls' boobs — even gay men appreciate them. So, I'll say it again: "EVERYBODY LOVES BOOBS." Now, there's obviously a debate in regards to size, shape, real, fake, and a bunch of other shit I don't really want to get into right now. Either way, regardless of your preference, boobs deserve your respect. In other words, if they aren't your boobs, don't be fucking touching them.

Take for example French physician René Théophile Hyacinthe Laennec. Not only was Laennec the inventor of the original stethoscope, he was a fucking professional and exemplary boob respecter. In 1816, Laennec didn't feel right putting his head up against a female patient's chest in order to examine her heart rhythm. (Why? Because he was fucking respectful — that's why.) So, he improvised and quickly fashioned together a sturdy tube consisting of several sheets of rolled paper. And, it worked. He could hear the beautiful rhythm of the patient's heart perfectly.

Laennec continued to improve upon his design, and the first documented use of his stethoscope was March 8, 1817. Oh, and he came up with the name "stethoscope" — Greek for, "I see the chest" — after getting tired of all the stupid names his friends were calling his invention. Eventually, decades of innovation led to the prop we now see used by non-qualified nurses and well-endowed doctors in today's medical-themed pornos. Congratulations, Laennec. Your device has truly come full circle.

Well, you just learned something new. You're welcome. Now, remember: It's okay to look — everybody does — but don't you dare touch them without permission, you pervy fucks.

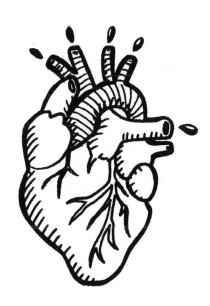

THE DENTIST OF DEATH

Alfred Southwick: steamboat engineer, mechanic, inventor, and dentist. Yeah, a dentist — what kind of sick fuck wants to be a dentist? Don't answer that.

Now, Alfred wasn't just your average dentist — because if he were — you wouldn't be reading about him today. You see, Alfred didn't just pull teeth and play with his pick all day; Alfred was the dude who invented the electric chair. I mean, who other than a fucking dentist would invent a chair that fucking kills you? The last time I went to the dentist, I wish someone would have fucking killed me.

Born in 1826, Alfred always had a knack for mechanical mischief. Shortly after graduating high school in Ohio, he moved to Buffalo, New York, where he began inventing dental tools. Again, who the fuck just wakes up one day and ponders, "Huh, you know what this world needs? More dental tools." God, this dude just keeps getting weirder and weirder.

Anyway, after successfully completing a dental apprenticeship at the not-so-young age of 36, Alfred became a dentist himself and opened his own practice. It was here that he perfected the art of strapping people to chairs and putting strange objects in their mouth. However, it wasn't until the year 1881 that Alfred got the idea for the electric chair. After hearing about some dumbass, drunk dude accidentally electrocuting himself to death, Alfred became intrigued by electricity and its deadly potential. (George was the name of the drunk dude who electrocuted himself, in case you were wondering.) Most people would hear that story and be like, "Oh shit, that's fucking . . . sad," but not Alfred. Alfred was like, "Oh shit, that's way cooler than cavities." So, as a former mechanic, Alfred got to work.

By 1888, he had the first electric chair prototype ready for action. And on January 1, 1889, the first law allowing death by means of electrocution went into effect in New York State.

So, the next time you're brushing your teeth with that electric toothbrush your dentist recommended, just know . . . if Alfred were still alive today, he'd probably find a way to make that toothbrush electrocute you to death.

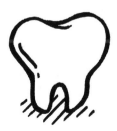

CARDIO IS FUCKING HARDIO

Cardio sucks. Running is meant for survival, not enjoyment. Running is a skill that we, as humans, developed to escape scary shit — like dinosaurs and marriage. Nobody "likes" running, so don't be one of those people who says they do. Because not only will everybody think you're an idiot, they'll also know you're a fucking liar. NOBODY likes running.

Can running possibly get any worse? Unfortunately, it can. Running at a gym on a treadmill is probably the closest thing you'll ever experience to Hell on Earth. You basically take all the shit that sucks about running, then you combine it with extreme bouts of boredom, other humans, and crappy ventilation. Oh, and then there's that weird, space-time continuum thing where you get temporarily trapped in an alternate treadmill universe — a universe where every minute feels like a fucking hour. So why are treadmills so awful? It's simple. It's because treadmills were designed for punishment.

The first treadmill was invented in 1818 by English engineer Sir William Cubitt after noticing most of the inmates in local prisons spent the majority of their time just standing around, hanging out, and well, not really being punished for their crimes. His initial invention was a series of steps that rotated at a slight angle around a vertical pole, replicating an endless staircase. These were installed in several prisons and used throughout the 19th century for two reasons: punishment and production. Prison treadmills were rigged to punish, but also harness the motion created by sweaty inmates to grind grain, collect water, and do other millworky-type things. Get it? "Tread," another word for walk or stride, plus the word "mill," to represent the work that was being done — and you have "treadmill." (Personally, I think "Endless Staircase of Death" would have been equally as appropriate for his creation. But what do I know? I'm a writer, not an engineer.)

Anyway, eventually some dude noticed how ripped all the prisoners were getting and realized that treadmills were probably good for weight loss, health, and other things. So the first patent for a "training machine" was issued in 1913.

Now, if you woke up early today to go running, good for you — as long as you admit it fucking sucked.

HATERS GONNA HATE

Don't you just hate it when someone asks you to "prove" something? I mean, not only are they calling you a liar, they're also questioning your ability to defend yourself. Essentially, they are insulting you twice. The good news: This kind of scrutiny generally means you're really good at something. And no matter what it is — writing, performing, sports, looking hot — jealous people will always question anything that seems too good to be true. Ever heard of Niccolo Paganini? No? Well, that's too bad. You should probably stop watching reality TV shows and get some fucking culture in your life because Niccolo was perhaps the greatest violinist of all time.

Born in Northern Italy in 1782, Niccolo developed his musical prowess at a young age, and by 1813, he was regarded by many as the best violinist in European history. His legend created a cult-like following of fans. (I believe these are called "groupies.") He was the first real rock star, both on — and especially off — the stage. But ... what Paganini did with his private parts is really none of our business. Let's get back to the story at hand.

Niccolo was such a talented musician, that a vast majority of folks were convinced he wasn't human; thus began the rumor that he was actually the son of the Devil and his violin contained the soul of a woman he had killed and imprisoned inside. Yeah, pretty fucking ridiculous, but these rumors became so intense and widely believed, that in order to continue traveling and performing, Niccolo was forced to prove his humanity by publishing letters and birth documentation from his mother. After proving he wasn't the Son of Satan, he was allowed to continue jammin' out; but the belief that he was associated with the devil never really went away.

Honestly, so what if Niccolo's dad were the Devil, so long as Niccolo put on a good show — right? C'mon, nearly every successful name in music has dabbled in the dark arts at least once in their life. I mean, I've had songs I don't even like stuck in my head for more than 10 years. That's some goddamn witchcraft if you ask me.

Anyway, the moral of the story: If people doubt you, hate on you, and constantly seem to be "out to get you," it usually means you're doing something right — so keep that shit up.

LOOKIN' GOOD, HONEY

Sometimes you don't want to be the one who gets all the attention, because not all attention is good attention. The pharaohs of Ancient Egypt knew this, and you should too. You see, in order to direct undesired attention towards someone other than the royal majesty, pharaohs required servants to smear their own bodies in honey. And, I'm not talking about a quick dab of honey behind the ear. Servants were practically forced to bathe in sticky-icky — like a latex bodysuit of bee puke. So what was the reasoning for the head-to-toe, sugary rubdown? Well, it was so flies and other bugs would land on the servants and not the pharaoh. Thus, ensuring the pharaoh always looked fly — instead of being covered in flies. Servants were made into literal flytraps.

Now, going back to what I said earlier about not all attention being good attention, this is perfectly exemplified with groups of girls at bars and clubs around the world. Think about it, when you're out with your girlfriends, sometimes you just want to be left alone to have a good time. You don't want the attention of hovering, drunk bar flies (also known as "horny dudes"). But, like the pharaohs, cunning women have found a way to divert the bar bugs away from themselves and onto somebody else — usually one of their friends.

Allow me to illustrate an example using our friend Megan. For this story, we'll say Megan is the pharaoh of her girl squad. And, like a pharaoh, she's rather full of herself. But instead of glazing her friends in honey like a Christmas ham, Megan tells her friends certain outfits look really "cute" even though it's obvious Jenna and Stephanie are going to attract A LOT of undesired attention. So, while her friends are getting swarmed by polo shirts with ill-fated pickup lines, Megan is free to relax in the corner — looking like fucking royalty among a sea of friends with bad fashion sense and horrible taste in men. Well played, Megan . . . kind of fucked up, but still well played.

Well, now you have a sweet Egyptian honey fact to share on your next coffee date so you can appear more interesting. (Even though you're fresh off a nine-day Netflix bender and have completely forgotten how to participate in society.)

KNOW WHEN TO GO

Life is all about knowing when to accept reality, throw in the towel, and move on. Grudges, relationships, hard feelings — if something's toxic, acknowledge it, fucking drop it, and get on with your life. Don't be that sad, pathetic loser who can't get over things and is continually obsessing over what once was or could have been. Don't live your life in "maintenance mode."

What is maintenance mode? Maintenance mode is when someone falsely maintains hope of getting back together or getting even instead of getting over things. People do this all the fucking time. You know why your ex-boyfriend won't give your stuff back? He's in maintenance mode. Rather than accepting the reality that the relationship is fucking done, he's trying to "maintain" just enough contact to hopefully get back with you someday. Guys, this is the same reason your ex-girlfriend won't give you the results to last month's paternity test: She wants to maintain contact with you. Why do people do this to themselves? Just give your ex-girlfriend back her fucking crossbow and get on with things. Don't be like King Ludwig of 19th-century Bavaria, the dude simply didn't know when to call it quits and move the fuck on. And, he ended up destroying his life — losing his throne, his castle, and even the woman he was obsessing over.

In 1847, Ludwig met a stage dancer by the name of Lola Montez. Sure, she was pretty, but she was also an absolute fucking wreck with a history of dragging dudes along for the ride. Despite Lola's warning signs and tumultuous past, King Ludwig gave her a royal home, a royal salary, and even a royal title. Feeling entitled by all that Ludwig had bestowed upon her, Lola began to overstep her bounds, abuse her title, and shake shit up in all the wrong ways — pissing off the nobles, the royal family, and even the townsfolk — but Ludwig still kept her around. He couldn't move on, he was too fucking obsessed with her.

And, in 1848, just a year after meeting her, the lords of Bavaria forced King Ludwig to step down from his royal throne. If he wasn't going to get rid of Lola, they were going to get rid of him. And, they did. Then, Lola got rid of him as well. (Because nobody wants to date a has-been.) In the end, Ludwig lost it all by simply not knowing when to throw in the towel and move on to a healthier relationship.

Don't be a fucking dud. Don't hang on too long like King Lud.

SEXUAL SWORDPLAY

S-E-X. You know, knocking boots, tappin' ass, answering the bone phone — whatever you choose to call it, no topic in society is discussed as often as sex. As humans, we're simply obsessed with it. So, naturally, sexual innuendos have found their way into pretty much every aspect of life over the years. Albeit, some of these innuendos were made far more obvious than others.

For example, single girls in 19th-century Finland would attend parties wearing an empty sword or dagger sheath around their waist. The single men in attendance, well, they'd slip their sword into the sheath of whichever girl they were interested in "getting to know." The girl could then decide to either remove the sword and return it to the potential suitor, or let the sword stay and allow the man to take an actual stab at her. Oh, and they were also now engaged. Yeah, engaged. A sword in the sheath was a marriage proposal. How fucking lame of a proposal is that? Imagine going to a bar as a single female nowadays if this same dating ritual were practiced today; there is absolutely no fucking way you'd leave without a fiancé.

Your mom would be like, "So how did you guys meet?" And your answer, "Silly story, Mom. So I got drunk at a bar and I thought I was carrying the sword of this tall, handsome doctor I was talking to earlier in the night. So I didn't return it, but, yeah, it wasn't. So now, Kyle and I are engaged — surprise!"

And then your dad would be like, "Goddamnit, Lindsey." And you'd be married to some piece-of-shit wannabe DJ for the rest of your life. Terrible, just terrible.

Now, aren't you glad guys at bars are only trying to poke you with their dicks instead of actual swords? The latter sounds pretty fucking dangerous.

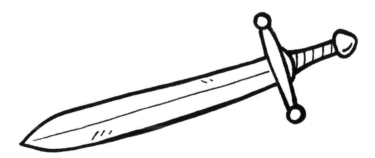

THE SMELL OF VICTORY

Making an entrance is fucking important. Trust me, there's a reason people continually stress the fact that you only get ONE first impression. Pretty much any time you decide to turn off Netflix and actually go interact with other humans is an opportunity to make a good one. You remember what humans are, right? Of course you do — you've seen them on Netflix.

Anyway, do you want to know who the literal queen of making an entrance was? None other than Cleo-Motherfucking-Patra. Yeah, she didn't just master winged eyeliner; she mastered pretty much every aspect of sensory seduction. And there's nothing more seductive or memorable than the sense of smell. For example: It's not the sight of a particular alcohol that will make you remember every aspect of your treacherous twenties — it's the smell. Cleopatra knew the nose knows long before scientists were running tests about scent recollection. So, before she set out on a diplomatic voyage in 41 B.C. to meet the Roman general, Mark Antony, she made damn sure his nose met her well before he did.

How did she do this? Well, in order to ensure she made the best first impression possible, Cleopatra had her ships adorned with beautiful, purple sails that were absolutely fucking soaked in her favorite perfume prior to taking sail. Thus, the same winds that would carry her boats to Rome, would also carry the scent of her perfume to the shore before her own arrival. Goddamn, say what you want about Cleopatra being a crazy snake lady, but she basically invented the art of arriving fashionably late.

I mean, when your scent gets there before you do, you're setting quite the stage for yourself.

And, well, it fucking worked. After catching wind of Cleo's arrival, Mark was head over heels for her days before her feet even touched Roman soil, and the two quickly became lovers and allies — forming the original "power couple."

So the next time somebody tells you that you're wearing too much perfume, tell 'em you're just allowing your reputation to precede you.

YOUR DOG KNOWS BEST

They say dogs can smell fear, but do you know what else they can smell? Bullshit. If your dog doesn't like somebody, it's because that person is a fucking loser. And if a dog doesn't like you, well, it's probably not the first time you've failed to make new friends. Humans have been using dogs as dickhead detectors for centuries. The Irish definitely did, and as early as the 5th century, they began adding the prefix "Cu" to the names of the noble kings and warriors who had proven themselves worthy of a dog's loyalty and affection. This way, you could immediately recognize the good guys because of their "Cu" title.

Take for example, Cu Chonnacht O'Reilly, Lord of Bréifne Ó Raghallaigh. In simpler terms, he was the King of Bréifne. Basically, this dude was a king who owned some badass dogs. And the "Cu" before his name means he had earned the trust, love, and affection of those badass dogs. Thus, he was a man you could trust. In other words, if you met a noble without the "Cu" before his name, he might be a cat owner and was somebody you should probably run from.

Basically, cat owners are fucking sketchy and the Irish knew this. You want to be a king? Get a fucking dog. You want people to love, honor, and respect you? Adopt a puppy. You want the world to know you're one of the good guys? Strut with your mutt. But, if you want to be a weird, sick lowlife, living in a small basement apartment — eating undercooked TV dinners while plotting the demise of your enemies — get a cat. Stroke it, talk to it, and together you can watch your evil plans fail, again and again. Nobody ever defeated their enemies with an animal that rhymes with mittens.

Well, there you have it. You just learned some hound history. So, the next time you meet someone who claims they're "not a dog person," report them to the authorities — immediately — because they're probably a terrorist.

PARISIAN PROSTITUTION

Transitioning to another kind of dog owner, like most great things, the French Bulldog is the result of selective breeding — kind of like the creation of Hot Pockets. Little bit of this, little bit of that, and eventually you end up with something wonderful. But, what you probably don't know about these stubby, little, bat dogs is they largely gained their popularity in the mid-1800s as the go-to accessory for socialites and streetwalkers to exude class, and thus, attract men. And, yes, streetwalker means prostitute. If you ask me, these ladies were fucking smart. Nobody can resist a French Bulldog. Everybody — man, woman, or beast — is going to approach you if you have one of these little dudes on a leash. And, that created the perfect opportunity to seal the deal and make a little money. French Bulldogs were basically the working girl's wingman.

Given the information I just presented about 19th-century French culture, it was safe to assume that if you saw a lady walking down the street with her hot pocket creation of a dog, there was a pretty good chance — with a little bit of money and some sweet talking — you could negotiate your way into her "hot pocket." Now, fast-forward to today, I'm not saying every girl who owns a French Bulldog is a hooker, but there's a pretty good chance she is. I'd say, something like 80/20. The 20 percent being the girls that are just trying to look rough around the edges — it's called streetwalker chic. And you know what? I love it. Because, as humans, we all have two basic needs: The need to pet dogs, and the need to touch butts. So for that reason, any girl that owns a French Bulldog is a girl I'd like to know.

DISCLAIMER: It's totally not my fault if you get punched in the dick for approaching a girl with a French Bulldog assuming she's a prostitute. Times have changed (I think).

DON'T LOSE SIGHT OF YOURSELF

Ladies, there's absolutely no guy in this world worth losing your shit over. There's no reason to get jealous, obsessive, and allow yourself to become insecure. If a guy doesn't like you, who fucking cares? Find one who does. If your boyfriend or husband makes you feel like shit, he's fucking shit — bury his ass in a sandbox, forget about him, and move on. Don't be like Joanna of Castile. Don't ruin your life and your reputation over some guy. Now, let's learn about Joanna.

Born in 1479, Joanna (Spanish spelling, "Juana") was the third child of Queen Isabella of Castile and King Ferdinand II of Aragon. Although she was born into privilege, that didn't stop her from working hard to improve herself. As a young woman, she spoke six languages — including Latin — excelled in religious studies, was active in equestrian sports, played music, and could dance with the best of them. Plain and simple, Joanna was a fucking badass. She was smart AND beautiful; this obviously attracted the attention of men. And, in 1496, she married Philip of Habsburg, also known as "Philip the Handsome." Seriously, the dude's nickname was PHILIP THE HANDSOME — are you fucking kidding me? He must have looked like Ryan Gosling and David Beckham had a baby. My point, even Philip's handsome ass wasn't worth losing her shit over. But, Joanna couldn't resist, she let her imagination get the best of her and she became absolutely paranoid he was going to cheat.

Joanna's insecurities continued to intensify and her mental instability grew evermore apparent around the kingdom. She was like a fucking vulture, constantly swarming over Philip, checking his iPhone, and demanding his email passwords. (They obviously didn't have that stuff back then, but if they did, that's what she would have been doing.) Needless to say, it was sad to watch. She was once such a smart, intelligent, confident woman. Not even Philip's surprise death in 1506 quelled her insecurities. She wouldn't allow nuns to approach his corpse before his burial — afraid he'd put his ghost boner in one of them.

In the end, Joanna of Castile became known as "Joanna the Mad." Leaving behind a reputation of being pathetically jealous, instead of beautifully badass.

ASHLEY'S FAKE EYELASHES

Jealousy. It's a hell of a thing. There is literally no other human emotion quite like it. It's powerful, it's sickening, and it causes people to do some ridiculous shit. Destroyed marriages, broken friendships, shattered careers — people will completely fuck up their lives over stupid feelings of envy, anxiety, and resentment. Guys are jealous of another guy's car, girls are jealous of another girl's guy, and everybody is jealous of somebody with great eyes and eyelashes.

Yeah, you heard me. Don't act like you don't wish your eyes were fucking pretty. Yes, even you, Mr. Macho Man, you know you'd blink the shit out of Paul Walker eyes if you had them. (R.I.P.)

People say eyes are the window to the soul, but that's some bullshit. Eyes are more like the doorway to your dreams. Seriously, if you have a sweet set of peepers — and you know how to use them — you can pretty much write your ticket in life. You can brainwash people with your baby blues and get yourself into all sorts of fun and/or trouble. You can even bounce from bedroom to bedroom if you're into that sort of thing, because everybody wants to have sex with a pretty-eyed stranger.

Speaking of sexy eyes, the Ancient Romans believed eyes — in particular, the eyelashes — were directly related to how much sex a person was having. Long eyelashes? She's a good, wholesome gal saving herself for marriage. Short, thin, ragged eyelashes? You better believe that girl is homie hopping. In fact, Pliny the Elder once said, "Eyelashes fall out from excessive sex, and so it is especially important for women to keep their eyelashes long to prove their chastity." Ha, now that's some bullshit. However, it was this belief that contributed to the invention of fake eyelashes and eye makeup . . . yeah, fake limbs for your eyelids have been around since Ancient Rome.

Well, there you have it, now you know why your friend Ashley refuses to leave the house without her fake eyelashes — she's just trying to look like Roman marriage material. *"Lookin' good, Ash."*

NO CHILD THANKS TO CROCODILES

Let's be honest, condoms suck. Nobody likes them. Not your mom, not your dad, not even the lady in your building living in 6E. (Yes, even Carol hates getting it with the use of a dick mitten.) But, sadly enough, condoms work. They keep your junk from burning, your crotch from itching, and most importantly, your life from falling apart. Because unless you're absolutely ready for it, pregnancy is a soul-crushing experience.

Accordingly, people have been finding ways to avoid the destructive nature of children long before the invention of the weenie glove. Even as far back as 1850 B.C., a time when the Ancient Egyptians got rather creative and resourceful with crocodiles. Yes, crocodiles. Toothy, reptilian, ferocious creatures — you know, like your boyfriend's ex-girlfriend. And with anywhere from 60-72 teeth and a 4,000-lb bite force, I would imagine putting your dick in a crocodile's mouth is pretty fucking awful . . . again, probably similar to the blowjobs given by the girlfriend before you. (God, you are just so much better than her, right?)

Anyway, the Ancient Egyptians made good use of the plentiful Nile crocs when it came to keeping a baby out of your lady box. So, how exactly did the Egyptians use the crocodiles? Well, it's actually quite simple. (Fucking gross, but simple.) They mixed crocodile dung, mud, and honey together to create an all-natural, highly effective spermicide. The pH level of crocodile dung will pretty much kill any little swimmer trying to find a home. First, I don't even want to know how the fuck the Egyptians figured that out.

Second, the first lady to volunteer to cover her vagina in crocodile shit, mud, and honey must have been into some seriously kinky stuff.

Now, remember, pregnancy is never a good game plan to lockdown a guy. In fact, you shouldn't let any guy wearing cargo shorts even near your lady parts. (That's probably the easiest way to avoid getting pregnant because it automatically eliminates 99% of all men.) But, the 1% of men without cargo shorts, might be worth risking it. Because they're most likely doctors or have some other career that requires them to respect themselves.

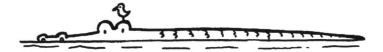

JAILHOUSE WEDLOCK

Weddings, birthdays, graduations, holidays — these milestone moments bring together family. A chance to gather, eat, and dodge the inevitable "So, why aren't you married yet . . . " question you'll be asked by relatives you forgot even existed. As if you weren't already self-conscious enough about your dating life, now you have people who are complete fucking strangers 364 days of the year questioning your "dateability." Who the fuck does Aunt Linda think she is anyway? She's been divorced four fucking times; she's the last person who should be questioning you. Regardless, she's doing it — so how do you answer? Well, it should begin by expressing the fact that you're just waiting for the "right guy." You know, one of those timeless, romantic moments that can only happen in a city like Paris, France.

The year is 1719, and dozens of so-called "undateable" women are about to meet the man of their dreams, get married, and be sent on an all-expenses-paid honeymoon to America. Because this is the year the French government offered male prisoners release if they agreed to do one simple thing as a condition of their liberation: Marry a prostitute and move to Louisiana. Yeah, even the French knew marriage is a punishment worse than prison. Pretty fucking romantic though, right? I mean, you had all these working girls, who had likely given up on finding a guy, suddenly married to a prison-sculpted, hard bod — some real "Pretty Woman" kind of shit. (No wonder Paris is known as "The City of Love.")

Now, it wasn't just criminals and call girls being sent to Louisiana (chained together, by the way — a literal "ball and chain" type of marriage); the government also sent the homeless, some families even sent their troubled teens. Essentially, deportation to Louisiana was done in an attempt to clean up the city. All in all, hundreds of Parisians became southern state castaways during the early 1700s . . . but, hey, at least some ladies got a husband out of it.

So, the next time they ask, let your relatives know you're just waiting for a French felon to come sweep you off your feet. Then, with a mouthful of mashed potatoes, share this story with them. There's still hope for you.

A HAIRY PROPOSITION

Everybody enjoys a good hat. The convenience of leaving your home without feeling the need to fuck with your hair beforehand is just awesome. But back in 19th-century Victorian Britain, the men didn't just wear hats to cover their hair — they wore hats to show off their lover's hair. Yeah, you read that right. Doesn't seem to make sense, does it?

Let's try it this way, there was actually a time when giving someone a chunk of your crotch wig was considered a sign of affection. A sign of affection men proudly displayed, pinning their lover's pubic hair to their hat like a trophy. (Perfectly reasonable. If you go to third base, you want to bring back a souvenir.) The best part about this was you'd never have to wonder if the carpet matched the drapes; you'd know for sure what everyone had going on — hat hair tells no lies. Plus, for girls, it would be super easy to catch your dude cheating on you. It would happen like this, "Karl! Whose fucking clam hair is this pinned to your hat!? These aren't my curls, you two-timing son of a bitch!" And, just like that, your marriage is over. (Karl, you fucking jerk.)

Anyway, chances are you have trouble even getting your boyfriend to wear that shirt you bought him last Valentine's Day. Now, imagine trying to get him to wear a tuft of pubes on his head. Now THAT would be a true measure of his love. You should probably ask him to do it. And I'm talking real pubes — not that shitty attempt at a beard he already has on his face.

If dudes 150 years ago could wear biscuit whiskers to show their commitment, surely your boyfriend can do it. It's so much more meaningful than a name tattoo. Trust me, I have one of those, and Ashley doesn't mean a thing to me.

STEP YOUR GAME UP

Girls love surprises. Think outside the bin with your next romantic gesture. Seriously, what the fuck is your girlfriend going to do with a 52-inch teddy bear anyway? C'mon, use your imagination for something other than dreaming about a rap career for once. Your poor girl has been putting up with your shit for months — maybe even years — and all you can do is get her something from the front bin of your local Walmart? That's just wrong.

Let's set the bar with a historical example of a dude going all-in for his girl: The year is 1931, and King Edward VIII (at this time, he was just Prince Edward) meets a married American woman by the name of Wallis Simpson. They hit it off, they frequent the bone zone together for a number of years, and Edward is convinced she is "the one." Wallis, feeling equally as passionate, obtains a divorce and gets ready to put her wifey lock on Edward's royal cock. At this same time, in early 1936, Edward's dad dies and Prince Edward becomes King Edward. Now, this is where it gets complicated.

Edward and Ms. Simpson's little arrangement is met with heavy opposition by the British government on all kinds of legal, political, religious, and moral grounds. The gist of it: As King of England, Edward was not allowed to marry a divorced woman because it was against the beliefs of the Church of England. So, what did Edward do? He gave up his throne. Yeah, the dude gave up his position as THE KING OF

MOTHERFUCKING ENGLAND just so he could marry Ms. Simpson. And, the two lived the remainder of their lives together in the beautiful French countryside.

Now, Edward may have given up his position as King of England — but in terms of romantic gestures — Edward will always be the King. In other words, *"Step your game up, teddy-bear boy."*

ROMANTIC REVENGE

Guys and lesbians, if you're lucky enough to land yourself a badass girl, you better hold onto her. Hold onto her like the way you clutch a 100-dollar bill, a gift card to your favorite restaurant, or anything else you find as important as food and money. Because you know what they say, "You don't know what you have until it's gone."

So, just how does one go about finding one of these elusive, unwavering creatures of badassness? Online dating? Nope. (Well, unless you want to date your fucking cousin or someone you went to high school with — equally disgusting options.) Your best bet is probably going to be in person. Perhaps through a friend of a friend, but most likely, it will happen when you least expect it. You might even die before you have a chance to realize how badass your girl really is. Take for example, Jeanne de Clisson, also known as "The Lioness of Brittany."

If that nickname doesn't prove just how badass this woman was, let me tell you a little more about her: In 1330, Jeanne married Olivier de Clisson IV, a wealthy Breton lord and son of a military legend. And, like all political couples, Olivier and Jeanne were under constant, almost-unfair scrutiny. In fact, in 1343, this resulted in Olivier being arrested by his own countrymen regarding a previous conflict he'd had with the English. He was put on trial, found guilty, and beheaded on August 2, 1343. (Yeah, there wasn't much of an appeal process back then.)

Appalled by the unjust treatment and execution of her beloved husband, Jeanne swore to avenge his death. So, she purchased three ships, painted them black, dyed the sails blood red, and became a fucking pirate. She then hired a crew along with two sons she shared with Olivier, and together, the family pursued and captured French fleets. (Way better than a family road trip.) As each new ship was captured, Jeanne would board their vessel and proceed to personally chop the French nobles' heads off with a fucking axe — a tribute to the same way French nobility had killed her husband.

Now, if you're debating about whether or not you should marry your current girlfriend, ask just how far she's willing to go to avenge your death. That's a great test of badassness. And, if you have yourself a Jeanne, you better get that girl a ring.

KEEP IT PRIVATE

Couples. They're disgusting. They're always kissing, sitting on the same side of a booth, sharing entrées, finishing each other's sentences, wearing matching outfits, using pet names, and a multitude of other obnoxious, PG-rated acts of love. Seriously though, if you're going to get down with some public displays of affection, at least make it worth watching for the rest of us. Either make me horny, or make your way into a car and go the fuck home — you cute, gross, disgusting lovebirds.

But whatever you do, don't go fighting and arguing in public, because there's nothing more uncomfortable or inappropriate than airing your dirty laundry in front of an audience. And, yes, social media does count as "in public." Besides, you're probably arguing about some dumb, boring, couple shit anyway. Speaking of that, I feel it's my duty to inform you — there are no rules when it comes to jumping ahead to the next episode of a series you started together. There's no "together" when it comes to binge watching, binge drinking, or binge eating; it's every man, woman, or gender-neutral individual for themself.

You know who's great at keeping their arguments quiet? Mimes. You know who else was great at this? Thomas Fucking Edison. (Yeah, the light bulb guy.) You see, after Thomas married his second wife, Mina Miller, in 1886, he taught her Morse code so they could communicate with finger tapping while holding hands. Allowing them to have a private conversation in a crowded room. It was kind of like texting when you're sitting right next to each other, except way cooler because it's fucking Morse code and it requires you to actually be smart and not just own a smartphone. My point, Thomas Edison was a smart guy. And, as a smart guy, he knew not everybody needed to hear his private conversations with his wife. You should do the same thing. Be smart. Be like Thomas and keep your relationship between the two of you.

Now, enjoy the rest of your day and start practicing your Morse code. Doing so would give the phrase "tap that" an entirely new meaning in your relationship.

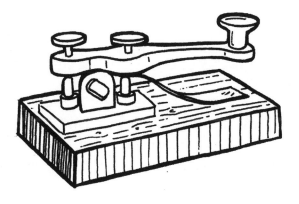

A PROVOKING SMOKE

There's nothing in life worse than feeling "controlled." Whether it's your boss telling you to stop dyeing your hair blue, or your bossy boyfriend/ girlfriend telling you to unfriend someone on Facebook — being told how to act is annoying. For example, if I were a dog, I wouldn't do a damn thing my owner told me. If he said, "Go fetch," I'd be like, "Go fuck yourself." Then I'd go chew a hole in his new sofa. Plain and simple, being told what to do fucking sucks. Unfortunately, this isn't something you can avoid. People and organizations will always attempt to control you in some way or another — and THAT is out of your control. But, you can ALWAYS control how you react. The way you react to someone telling you what you can, or cannot do, is completely up to you.

Take for example Katie Mulcahey. On January 22, 1908, Ms. Mulcahey was arrested in New York City's Bowery district for smoking a cigarette in public. Which, at the time, was illegal under the Sullivan Ordinance. A dumb law created by some lame-ass, self-righteous union to ban women — and only women — from public inhalation. They believed smoking was immoral and had the law passed in order to preserve the purity of NY's female populace. And, in all her impure glory, Katie broke that law.

And this is what she said to the judge, "I've got as much right to smoke as you have. I never heard of this new law, and I don't want to hear about it. No man shall dictate to me." Well, the judge didn't really like the feeling of his balls shriveling up inside him, so Katie was found guilty and fined five dollars (roughly $150 today). But, Katie didn't give a fuck. She was just getting started.

In fact, she stirred up enough shit after the verdict to garner the attention of the mayor. So, just two weeks after Katie's arrest, the mayor vetoed the anti-smoking law and women were once again allowed to get their smoke on.

Fuck "Columbus Day." Where's our "Katie Mulcahey Day" — right?

Now, the next time somebody tries to tell you what to do — like your server telling you you've had too many brunch mimosas — think to yourself, "W.W.K.D.," then use your best outside voice to say, "I'll tell you when I've had enough."

CRAZY LADY BAY

A lot of girls like to joke about being a handful, but the truth is: You probably fucking are. Fortunately, there are plenty of dudes who dig the shit out of girls slightly off their rocker. There's something oddly rewarding about being able to handle a girl no one else can. It's like being a pirate, and crazy girls are like an ocean — full of sharks, saltwater crocodiles, jellyfish, and a bunch of other shit that will totally fucking kill you — but, if you know how to navigate her deadly, crazy-lady waters, you'll reach an island filled with treasures. Treasures like: exciting conversations, R-rated movies, and sex on a Tuesday. Sounds awesome, right? Of course it does.

Granted, dating a lady like this requires a man to always maintain a good sense of humor about life — a life she will gladly end if he's not careful. Take for example the great German poet Heinrich Heine. You see, in 1830 (some say 1831), Heinrich left Germany and moved to Paris because the German government wasn't exactly fond of his controversial writing. In fact, shortly after his voluntary departure, the government banned him from ever returning. So what? He was in Paris — way cooler anyway. It was here that he met a young woman named Crescence Eugénie Mirat. Now, keep in mind, Heine was a German poet, Crescence didn't speak any German, and she had absolutely no interest in reading or writing. She was pretty much the exact opposite of everything he lived for. So, he didn't exactly choose a woman who would be easy to deal with. But they made it work, and they were married in 1841. They stayed together until

Heinrich's death in 1856. And, in his will, we get a taste of the sense of humor that was necessary to make their relationship work all those years.

In that will, Heinrich left her all of his wealth, but with a catch: She had to remarry in order to receive it. Why did he want her to remarry? Because in Heinrich's words, "Then there will be at least one man to regret my death." You see, Heine knew his wife was a pain in the ass and thought it would be funny to watch another man try to deal with her shit. Anyway, she quickly remarried. You know, because money is cool and stuff. But I'm sure he floated around as a ghost on all her first dates like, "Oh no he didn't."

Anyway, dudes, don't let anybody — not even a fucking ghost — stop you from sailing into Crazy Lady Bay. It's totally worth it.

GET IT, GIRL

Like coming between a bear and her cubs, coming between a girl and her goals is a recipe for fucking disaster. Whether it's the pursuit of a career goal, or much-needed carbohydrates, if a woman's mind is set on something, it's fucking on. And, in recent times, I can't think of a goal-driven woman who brought it harder than Emmeline Pankhurst, a revolutionary leader of the British women's suffrage movement.

Following the death of her husband in 1898, Emmeline was left a single mother of five. Her husband had always been her strongest supporter, but now, without him, she was forced to pursue her dream of equal voting rights for British women on her own. So in 1903, she formed the Women's Social and Political Union.

Now, one important thing to note about Emmeline, she wasn't about clever rhymes and picket signs. She was a woman of action who lived by the motto, "Deeds, not words." What kind of deeds exactly? Well, in 1912, Emmeline was arrested 12 times for arson, vandalism, and other hoodrat things she did to bring attention to her fight. TWELVE FUCKING TIMES — in ONE year. Your favorite rappers don't have shit on Emmeline's level of street cred. With her background, she could have easily dropped a mixtape if she so chose. Something like — "Guilty of Being a G" — would have been an appropriate title.

I mean, talk about a woman who literally did not give a fuck. Not even one. In a court appearance following one of her arrests, she said, "We are here not because we are lawbreakers; we are here in our efforts to become lawmakers." You see what I'm saying about never getting in the way of a determined woman and her goals? No matter what, she never lost sight of her goal. All she wanted was equal voting rights, and she fought for that goal until the day she died: June 14, 1928, at the age of 69. (Ha, classic. Sixty-nine — even her death age was rebellious.) And, just weeks after her death, the Equal Franchise Act was passed, allowing all British women over 21 to vote, regardless of property and marital status.

So, the next time you and your friends can't decide on where to eat, TAKE A VOTE. If you're not happy with the outcome, do what Emmeline would do and set something on fire.

FIGHTING FOR THE RIGHT

"Free the nipple." You've seen the hashtag, you've read the posts — and you know what — I'm totally on board with it. Why? Duh, because nipples are fucking cool; they're second only to side boob. (Side boob wins every time.) The way I see it, if you're happy with the size, shape, and spacing of your milk duds, you should definitely be allowed to share them, when and wherever you want (if that's your thing). It's a personal choice. Unfortunately, it's a choice only reserved for men. Which is wrong, because dude nipples are fucking dumb and ugly. You can't even milk a dude. (Yeah, your boyfriend really is fucking worthless.) However, there was a time when even men weren't allowed to expose their gumdrops in public.

The Civil War wasn't the only war fought on North American soil. The Nipple Wars of the 1930s were equally as brutal, but involved far less bloodshed. Let's hear about one of these terrifying battles and the brave men who fought for the right to party with your shirt off. The year was 1936, and it was a particularly hot day up in America's toupee, a.k.a. Toronto, Canada. So hot that many men decided to bare their chests at a local beach (fucking rebels). This rogue move resulted in 30 men being arrested for "indecent exposure." I mean, I've heard of some pretty weird shit coming out of Canada — like polite criminals and affordable healthcare — but this story really takes the Canadian Cake.

FYI - A "Canadian Cake" is a slang term I just made up for a birthday party that involves beer, fistfights, and pouring brown gravy on FUCKING

EVERYTHING. (Canadians will get it.) Now, in Canada's defense, men were fighting the same fight in New York City at that time as well. Basically, in 1936, we were all prudes.

Anyway, shortly after the Toronto Titty Gang members were arrested, the laws were changed and it was finally deemed acceptable for men to go topless. Thus, the first major victory of the North American Nipple Wars was won.

Fast-forward to today, what's so offensive about female nipples anyway? I say, "Free the female nipple, hide the fucking bro toes." If you want to talk about something offensive, let's talk about dudes wearing sandals . . . fuck flip-flops.

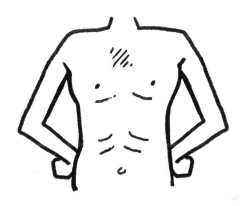

LAWS, LIARS, AND LIBATIONS

Dudes will say just about anything to get laid. Absolutely relentless with unoriginal compliments, career lies, and anything else they think will help them get horizontal. Any woman who's left her house long enough to go to a bar, club, or pet store knows what I'm talking about. Shit like, "I don't usually talk to girls at bars," "I'm not like other guys," and "I read books." Lies, lies, lies — he just wants a piece of your cherry pie. (Sorry, that was gross. Calling a vagina a cherry pie sounds like a time-of-the-month metaphor.)

Anyway, the tactic of lying for lady bits — also referred to as "spitting game" — is as old as time. Your dad did it to your mom and Adam probably did it to Eve. (I don't think her leaf just fell off.) At one point, laws were even passed in an attempt to prevent this behavior by making it illegal for men to bullshit their way into bed. Known as "Anti-Seduction Acts," or "Seduction Laws," states such as New York, Virginia, Ohio, and Georgia passed these ordinances during the 1800s. Each state had its own take on seduction policy, but the one thing they all had in common: Seduction Laws applied to the false promise of marriage . . . ha, really? How fucking desperate is that? One minute he's buying you a drink and lying about his career as an astronaut, the next, he's throwing out the mother of all Hail Marys and asking for your hand in marriage.

Now, the really stupid thing about these laws, they assumed women couldn't already sniff out some bullshit. Like, somehow, a false marriage proposal was a hypnotic guarantee of gettin' some. I don't know about you, but I'm pretty sure girls don't need legal legislation to help them avoid a douche. I mean, I've spent a fair amount of time in Las Vegas — and from what I've seen, women are perfectly capable of navigating douchey waters.

Girls, if a guy simply won't stop trying to get into your honey pot, you're in luck, because there's still a law for you: Newton's Law of Universal Gravitation. This law states, if you hold your drink above a man's head and rotate it sideways, the contents within will do the work of getting rid of him.

A MUTUAL UNDERSTANDING

"So, what are we?" The dreaded question nobody wants to hear from someone they think they're just *casually* dating. "Are you my friend, my fish friend, my girlfriend, or my half-fish friend who happens to also be a girl?" Yeah, dating a mermaid would be fucking confusing.

Now, I don't care whether you're a man, woman, or mythical sea harlot, discussing your expectations of a relationship is necessary. If you don't want something serious, just be honest about it. Don't let the other person think it's something it's not as they run around telling everyone the two of you are "dating" when really all you did was split an appetizer a few weeks back. One-sided relationships are bullshit and sad — like the very one-sided relationship between King George III of Great Britain and Elizabeth Spencer.

You see, King George was obsessed with Elizabeth. So obsessed that he one day decided he was no longer married to his actual wife, Queen Charlotte, and instead started telling everyone he was married to Elizabeth and Charlotte was a spy trying to kill him. Obviously, embarrassing the hell out of both women. The entire time, Elizabeth was probably like, "George, why are you so obsessed with me?" She literally wanted nothing to do with him, but that didn't stop George from telling everyone about their new relationship. It's worth mentioning that at this time George had also begun to suffer from a rare blood disease known as porphyria, causing him to experience bouts of severe dementia. (Makes sense. Because you literally have to be fucking insane to want to get married — twice.)

Anyway, long story short, porphyria eventually got the best of ole Georgie Boy several years later and he died on January 29, 1820. Leaving behind one real widow, and well, one fictitious one.

Clearly, not coming to a mutual understanding of what you are as a couple is just embarrassing and awkward for everyone involved.

BUCKET BRAWLERS

Admit it. If you're in a relationship, you fight about stupid shit. And, anything is fair game when it comes to arguing with your boyfriend or girlfriend: t-shirts, TV shows, toothbrushes — all valid fodder on a Thursday night. Couples are like angry magicians, but instead of pulling rabbits and doves out of thin air, they pull out topics to argue about. Why? Because humans have exceptional imaginations when they're in a relationship. This is why single people hate couples so much. It's not because we're jealous of your love, it's because we know that deep down inside we all possess the potential to become just like you — and we're fucking scared to death about it.

Now, if you're coupled up, you've probably already begun thinking about all the pointless stuff you've argued about this past week. Well, I'm about to one-up you when it comes to pointless combat. The year is 1325, and a war has just erupted between Modena and Bologna, two rivaling city-states in Northern Italy. Why are they fighting? Because of a bucket. Yes, a fucking bucket. You see, a group of drunk soldiers from Modena snuck into Bologna one night and stole the water bucket from the town well. And, well, the Bolognese people weren't about living a no-bucket life, so the war was fucking on.

All in all, "The Battle of Zappolino" — also known as "The War of the Bucket" — saw bloodshed of about 4,000 men. Making it actually one of the largest battles of the Medieval Era. And you thought your silly fights got serious . . . pfft. Did anybody die? Nope. So relax, your fights are basic.

However, much like the asinine arguments you have with your boyfriend or girlfriend, the bucket-stealing incident was simply the final straw and culmination of years of hostility and annoyance. So, the next time your boyfriend or girlfriend picks a stupid fight with you, try to understand it's most likely the apex of their annoyance about something else you've been doing for some time. Like, always making them sleep in the wet spot after your sloppy, post-argument, make-up sex. That's such a jerk move. You should definitely be taking turns snoozing in the postcoital puddle — or at least rock-paper-scissors for it . . . best out of three.

MAKE HIM WORK FOR IT

Vaginas are powerful. Let's be honest, women are basically walking around with an atomic bomb between their legs. And with that kind of power comes the ability to command absolute fear, respect, and devotion. Like Queen Njinga (alternate spelling, "Nzinga") of Angola did during her African reign in the 1600s. Her story begins during the height of the Portuguese slave trade.

Shortly after the death of her father, King Kiluanji, in 1618, her brother took to the throne, but his lack of leadership skills quickly became apparent. So, he simply gave up. He committed suicide in 1626, allowing the Portuguese to essentially do whatever the fuck they wanted with the Angolan population. And, well, Njinga wasn't about that life. So she took control, assumed the throne, and began her retaliation against the Portuguese. Her ruthlessly independent nature made her a brilliant military leader as she organized several guerrilla armies to defend her people. Her independent spirit also meant that instead of finding a man to become the new king, she simply took on the role herself, requiring that she be referred to as a "king" rather than "queen." And, like most kings did back then, she amassed herself a large harem: Hundreds of male concubines kept around solely for her sexual pleasure.

Now, you wouldn't expect a woman of her status to let just any dude wet his willy with her, would you? Of course not. So in order to find the right guy for the night, she'd choose two and watch them fight to the death.

The winner earned the honor of her royal attention. Then, in order to prevent him from getting too clingy, she'd have him killed the following morning. (Damn, not even breakfast or coffee. Harsh.) The pattern continued for nearly 40 years — fighting the Portuguese by day, watching dudes fight to have sex with her by night. Her life was like one of those sexy, violent Rihanna music videos.

Now, ladies, your vagina is kind of a big deal. I'm not saying you should make guys fight to the death for it, but you should definitely make them work a little. I don't know, maybe something involving karate, or better yet, a fucking career.

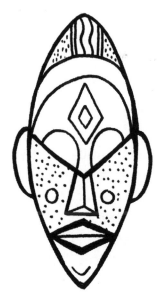

PET PARENTING 101

Sure, you can call yourself a "dog mom" or a "cat daddy," but the truth is, you're not a fucking parent — you're a kidnapper, and pets are the ultimate example of Stockholm syndrome. (If you don't know what that is, quickly Google it so we can get on with learning.)

I mean, when has your dog ever complained about where you live? Not once. You just randomly brought him home one day like, "Hey, welcome to your new home," and never has he said shit about your dirty laundry, wine-stained carpet, or poorly assembled IKEA furniture set. He simply accepted his new life with a good attitude and a happy tail. So, the way I see it, there's no such thing as taking it too far when it comes to being a good parent to your pets. I say, buy them cute clothes, throw them birthday parties, and treat them like a member of the fucking family. That's the least you can do after kidnapping them from their real mom. Just don't do what Mary Toft did . . . she was fucking crazy.

In 1726, the seemingly normal resident of Surrey, England, took the pet-parenting thing a little too far. You see, Mary Toft had such a weird-ass obsession with rabbits, she would actually stuff bunnies up her vagina and pretend to give birth to them. Literally trying to be their mom. (And you thought visiting your gynecologist was uncomfortable.) She even performed this feat in front of doctors, convincing them she was a legit bunny-birther. In fact, medical professionals began to attribute her miraculous conceptions to "maternal impression" — the belief that dreams and obsession could lead to physical changes within a mother's womb. After several doctors vouched for the validity of her story, she became an overnight celebrity and even caught the attention of the British royal family.

She carried on her hare hoax for months, giving birth to at least 15 bunnies during this time. It wasn't until a politician put her claims under intense investigation that she finally confessed to what she was doing. (Oh, I forgot to tell you, Mary was married this entire time. It was actually her husband who was buying all the bunnies for her to "birth.")

Huh, suddenly becoming a crazy cat lady doesn't seem so crazy, does it?

SQUAD GOALS

A girl squad is like a flock of birds: If you spook one, you spook 'em all. Basically, if you're dating one of them, you're pretty much dating all of them. Because every fight, every picture, every text — EVERYTHING you do (or do not do) — will become subject to the squad's ridicule, investigation, and approval. But it's not all bad. If you're a decent guy, your girlfriend's squad might actually be your greatest asset. If they like you, your girlfriend's friends will be your strongest advocates during those times when your girlfriend completely loses her fucking mind. Girls trust the shit out of their friends, and that's why girl squads exist.

Even great queens throughout history have relied on their squad to approve of potential suitors. Don't believe me? Let's learn more: Catherine the Great ruled Russia from 1762 until 1796, making her the longest running female leader in Russia's history. She was smart, savvy, sophisticated, and goddamn fierce. Under her rule and military command, Russia was established as a dominant power. (You're welcome, Russia. A lady did that. Now cheer the fuck up.) Anyway, you'd think a woman as powerful and smart as Catherine wouldn't need girlfriends for advice, right? Wrong. Catherine was a sex fiend. I'm talking freaky-deaky shit, but because of her position and reputation, she couldn't go around fucking just anybody — she was the Empress of Russia for God's sake. So, she enlisted the help of her squad.

In order to get to Catherine, you had to go through them. Literally. If Catherine thought you were hot, she'd ask you to sleep with a member of her squad first to make sure you were able to satisfy her own royal thirst. If you came up short, it was mission abort, and Catherine was on to the next one. (Damn, at least with a dick pic you get a few moments to explain yourself.)

Now, guys, I know it's a pain in the ass, but learn to play nice with your girlfriend's friends — you never know when you might need them on your side. Yes, even Ashley. (I know, I don't get it either. Ashley's a fucking mess . . . nobody should be taking advice from her.)

FEMALE FEROCITY

Take no shit. If somebody wrongs you, don't just sit back and let it happen. People treat you the way you allow them to treat you. If you continually roll over, they'll continue to roll over top of you like a truck. Whether it's work, a relationship, or simply your everyday life — if somebody doesn't treat you right, do something about it. Now, as a female, you'll probably be called a "bitch" every time you defend yourself, but guess what, it's better to be a bitch than a victim. So stick up for yourself and don't be afraid to get a little crazy — be like Hannah Duston.

Born in 1657, Hannah grew up in Massachusetts, where she lived a rather calm life until the year 1697. That year, the mother of nine was kidnapped by a group of raiding Abenaki during King William's War. But, this wasn't just your typical "Hey, check out my van" kind of kidnapping. This kidnapping was straight Eli Roth shit. Because not only did they burn Hannah's house down so her family had nowhere to hide, they also killed her newborn child right in front of her. All in all, around 27 colonists were axed, and 13 more taken captive during the one-night free-for-all. Granted, we know the early colonists did some pretty fucked-up shit and probably had this coming, but what Hannah did next is still impressive.

You see, Hannah wasn't about to just sit back and let them get away with all this. Hannah, like most moms, was a fighter. So that's what she did: fought. After days of being forced to march through the snow, she seized an opportunity to shake shit up as her captors were sleeping.

What exactly did she do? Well, she escaped her restraints, got ahold of an axe, and FLIPPED THE FUCK OUT — single-handedly killing 10 warriors, and sending the others running for the hills — you know, like your last boyfriend ran from the truth and responsibilities.

Now, if Hannah's not the definition of a "bad bitch," I honestly don't know what is. Following her rampage, she then helped the other captives escape and led them to a farmhouse, where they were able to seek shelter until they had the strength to make the 30-mile trek back home. (Talk about a shitty camping trip.)

So, the next time somebody wrongs you, don't be afraid to harness your inner Mrs. Duston and go absolutely apeshit. Also, this story proves something I was once told by a good friend: "Postpartum hormones are nothing to fuck with."

NACHO DADDY

Maybe your current girlfriend gave you the kick in the ass you needed to pursue a new job, maybe she provided you with the tough love you needed to stop being such a piece of shit, or maybe she's just really good at building up your manhood and making you believe your dick is bigger than it is — ultimately, leading to a better sex life. My point: A lot of good things in life wouldn't happen without men receiving the proper motivation (or inspiration) from their girlfriend, wife, and other women in their lives. And, here's fucking proof.

The year was 1943, and a young maître d' named Ignacio Anaya had no idea he was about to change history when a group of hungry, demanding military wives from Fort Duncan entered his restaurant in Piedras Negras, Mexico. What exactly happened? Well, on that particular day at the Victory Club, the chef was nowhere to be found. So, Ignacio, immediately recognizing how fucking dangerous a group of hungry women could be, knew that only he could prevent impending disaster. Not being one to shy away from a challenge, he stepped up to the plate.

He went into the back kitchen, found some tortilla chips, found some cheese, sliced some jalapeños, stacked everything together, threw it in an oven — and just like that — he became the father of nachos. Yep, it was that easy. Why the name nachos? Equally as easy: "Nacho" was Ignacio's nickname. (But after all this, I like to think women began calling him "Nacho Daddy." Something like, "Yeah . . . Yeah . . . Put your cheese right there, Nacho Daddy.")

I, for one, could not be more grateful for what these women inspired Ignacio to accomplish on that day, because I've never seen a nacho plate I didn't want to impregnate. Anyway, word of his creation eventually snuck across the border to Texas, where it quickly became a baseball stadium staple (you see, immigration is a good thing). Now, who knows, had it not been for those hungry women, mankind may have never invented nachos. We'd all be eating celery like a bunch of fucking idiots.

So, ladies, the next time you're hungry and giving your boyfriend attitude, let him know you're just trying to motivate him to actually do something with his fucking life — like Ignacio did when he fathered nachos.

THE PIRATE QUEEN

Traveling, drinking, fighting, and prostitution — just another day in the life of infamous Chinese pirate Captain Cheng I. (Let's not get into the differences of Cantonese and other Chinese dialects; I'm dramatically simplifying these names down for you.)

You see, Cheng commanded one of the largest documented pirate fleets in history, ransacking much of the South China Sea he called home. But, even Cheng wanted more from life, so in 1801, he married a prostitute who went by the name "Cheng I Sao." Basically, "Wife of Cheng." Not only was she fucking gorgeous, she was also equally as good at handling a sword as she was at handling a dick. Oh, and she was EXTREMELY business savvy. Together, the husband-and-wife team pillaged and plundered for six years. Expanding their joint empire until the year 1807, the year Captain Cheng died.

Was this the end of their pirate dynasty? Nope, it was only the beginning. Cheng I Sao assumed the leadership role and picked up right where her husband had left off. Only now, she was going by the name "Ching Shih" because she was no longer somebody's wife.

Ching Shih continued to build her empire with brute force and sharp wit. She also played dudes like the dumbasses they are when around an attractive woman. (You know, like smart bartenders and servers do.) And, within a few years, Ching Shih became the most powerful pirate in history — controlling more than 1,500 ships and a crew of 80,000 men.

She was like Beyoncé, but with street cred and more boats. In fact, she was so smart and so powerful that the Chinese government eventually gave up trying to defeat her. In 1810, the government offered her complete amnesty if she would simply retire. So, she did. As part of the deal, she was allowed to keep all her money, all her fame, and all her power. (Remember what I said earlier about her savvy business sense?)

After retiring, Madame Ching opened a gambling house and just chilled until 1844, dying at the age of 69 as a grandmother and certified badass.

Anyway, remember this story the next time a guy tells you, "It's a man's world."

HELL IN HEELS

You like scary stories? Good, me too. Allow me to share one of my favorites with you. Are we going to talk about ghosts? Nope. The Loch Ness Monster? Thought about it, but couldn't find any trustworthy sources. Children? Definitely creepy, but that's a lesson for another day. I know what you're thinking, "Captain, what could possibly be scarier than ghosts, the Loch Ness Monster, and children?" Well, I'm about to tell you: feet. Yep, the hand's awkward stepsister. Thank God you can hide (or at least accentuate) those disgusting ankle abominations with socks, footed pajamas, rollerblades, and most importantly, shoes. In particular: high heels.

Stilettos, peep toes, ankle straps, sling backs — it doesn't matter to me — I support that life, and any other shopping addiction that helps you hide your fucking toes. Hell, I don't even mind seeing a guy wearing heels. In fact, I might even throw a compliment or two his way, "Sweet calves, bro." A calf compliment is rather appropriate because calves (and other cattle) fit seamlessly into this high-heeled tale I'm about to tell you.

Why? Because high heels were originally invented by Egyptian butchers to keep their feet clean as they walked through the blood pools of slaughtered beasts. Yes, long before heels were being worn by drunk girls stumbling through piles of club confetti, Egyptians were wearing them to power walk through blood and guts. This backstory might explain why your girlfriend often feels the need to use her shoes as a weapon. It also doesn't hurt that the word "stiletto" is taken from a style of knife blade made popular in Italy during the Middle Ages.

Huh, so high heels were invented by butchers, and later named after a fucking weapon? Suddenly everything's starting to make sense.

Dating back to 3500 B.C. (some records indicate as early as 4000 B.C.), the original Egyptian heels were more reminiscent of the modern-day wedge. The more traditional version of high heels were first worn by Mongolian horsemen, and later, cavalry riders during the Middle Ages because the heels helped them secure their feet into the stirrups (kind of like cowboy boots). Imagine that, Genghis Khan, one of the most ruthless motherfuckers of all time, riding into your town wearing some red bottoms. Even if he decided not to burn down your village, his smoldering hot sense of fashion would certainly have been enough to start a fire.

Anyway, royalty (a.k.a. "old-timey celebrities") eventually started wearing heels as a fashion statement. And the rest is, well, *fucking history* . . .

ABOUT THE AUTHOR

Writer. Creator. Instigator. Not your dad.

@SGRSTK

MORE TITLES FROM THE CAPTAIN:

'NOTHERFUCKING HISTORY

FEEL FREE TO QUOTE ME

FEEL FREE TO QUOTE ME AGAIN

Made in the USA
San Bernardino, CA
16 December 2019